Craigmillar Gold

songs from the community musicals

volume one: 1973-77

Craigmillar Gold

songs from the community musicals
volume one: 1973-77

Edited by: Douglas Galbraith

Research: Heather Henderson

Music assistant: Susan Wilson

ARTS: THE CATALYST

CRAIGMILLAR

This book is dedicated to Faye Milligan,
who appeared in every musical since 1973, except one,
until her untimely death in 2003.

Published in 2004 by the Craigmillar Communiversity Press

ISBN 0-9543348-3-3

This book was possible because of the support of Awards for All
Heritage Lottery and Craigmillar Capacity Building

 The proceeds from the sale of this book and accompanying compact disc go towards supporting future voluntary projects through the Craigmillar Communiversity.

From the archive of Johnni Stanton, Alice Henderson, Steve Burgess and Helen Crummy

This publication is part of the 'Arts: the Catalyst' Exhibition,
at the City Arts Centre, Edinburgh, from 29 October until 31 December 2004.

Book and cover design: Mark Blackadder

The music is set in Music Publisher 5, Braeburn Software, Selkirk (sales@braeburn.co.uk)

Printed and bound in Scotland by Hugh K. Clarkson & Sons Ltd.

Introduction

The Craigmillar Festival Society, active from the nineteen-sixties until the closing years of the twentieth century, was a group of local residents committed to tackling the problems of an area of the city lacking in amenities and with more than its fair share of social deprivation. Believing it was 'the poor who know best the problems of the poor', they sought partnership with government in projects to improve the physical environment as well as the educational and social opportunities available to residents. From the beginning, its conviction was that the starting point for such social and political action should be in community arts for, unless young and old were enabled to find their identity and unlock the talents each had, true community renewal could not take place. In time, there developed the annual community musicals where not only were audiences and cast given a vision of what such a community might be like but participants enabled to discover their own potential.

During the 1970s and 80s, as the gaily painted play bus came over the Castle hill after a happy day spent on the beach, the grey streets of Craigmillar would suddenly fill with the joyous voices of children belting out with pride, Craigmillar now – fine place to be' … 'Rehabilitation' … 'More of us than you' and many other catchy tunes from the community musicals. The young grew up singing them, parents and grandparents learned them from the kids.

Craigmillar community musicals, often called our 'secret weapon', combined culture with satirical criticism. They were colourful and hilarious, based on the area's social concerns or historical events. Local people developed the scripts, and costumed and staged many spectacular productions. Among them *The Time Machine* (opposing the building of a motorway through the area), *Castle, Cooncil and Curse* (highlighting the area's 600 empty houses), *Willie Wynn* (the plight of a child growing up in a one parent family – 10% of Scottish children were at that time living in poverty), *Craigmillar Recipe* (threatened with the axe, the Festival Society gave its recipe for survival), *Shoo* (giving members of the EEC Poverty Programme who came from Brussels to see it the people's definition of real-life poverty).

The musicals were professionally directed by well known Scottish actors. Among those who came to Craigmillar to help were Bill Paterson, Kenny Ireland, Billy Riddoch, Jimmy Chisholm, Ronnie Letham, Katie Gardner, the late Victor Carin, Eileen McCallum, Sandy Neilson, Ian Woolridge, John Murtagh, Alan Waters, Ian Watson, and many others. During rehearsal periods, the director would visit schools, groups and senior citizen's clubs whose pupils or members were in the cast. Thus residents learned on the grapevine what was happening and, curious to see the actor in the flesh, would flock to the show, which, thanks to professional coaching from many of these actors, as the years went by, graduated from being a good amateur show to becoming near professional.

In addition, local minister Rev. Douglas Galbraith, who was Festival Music Director from 1973-77, was an inspiration to many. Not only did he write many of the lyrics and music, he gave countless young people the confidence to play and compose, encouraging and developing their musical potential and giving them lifelong pleasure.

In addition to playing on the Festival Fringe, the shows were at times taken on tour, playing at various Glasgow and other Scottish venues, London's Caxton Hall and a never to be forgotten week's tour of Belgium and Holland as the guest of the Dutch Government. It is good to be reminded of these songs, and of the enthusiasm of the participants in these musicals, as we celebrate the place of the arts in the renewal of our communities.

Dr. Helen Crummy MBE
Organising Secretary, 1962–83
Newcraighill, October 2004

Preface

The exhibition, 'Arts: the Catalyst', celebrates the unique contribution the arts can make in community renewal, drawing on the experience of the Craigmillar Festival Society whose initiatives attracted much interest in both Scotland and overseas and from which similar projects drew inspiration and encouragement.

The songs in this volume are mostly from the first five full scale community musicals, a pattern which developed some years into the life of the Society. They come from the pen of some fourteen authors, nearly all local to Craigmillar and most of them young. The songs bear the signs of having to be written to order: to clothe a developing script (invariably having its genesis in the mind of the Organising Secretary Helen Crummy, one of the founding members of the Society), or for a particular group of participants, or to meet a deadline!

Most are included in this volume in whatever form they had managed to reach in time for rehearsal, when the bare signs on the page were given life by plot and by the enthusiasm of the performers. Some were scribbled down from memory for the first time after the show was over. All need interpreted, and the accompanying compact disc shows how vivacious singing could turn a very basic musical idea into a vehicle for an emotion or an idea, and how interpretation by a skilled performer could bring out what might be only dimly present in a composer's mind.

Many songs are in a keyboard version, others simple melody with or without guitar chords. This does not indicate the variety of accompaniment, from rock band to mediaeval instruments, which occurred in actual performance.

Thirty years on, some of the songs are still sung in Craigmillar. In later years, there were many more songs by many more composers. These may find their place in a second volume.

Contents

Helen Crummy and Bill Paterson

The Time Machine 1973

The 'time machine' was a bulldozer driving a threatened ring route through Craigmillar and its environs, not only demolishing buildings but destroying what had been a growing sense of community. Locals felt that, of the options before the planners, their district had been chosen as the most expendable.

Also in the path of the road was the seventeenth century mansion, 'Hermits and Termits', now derelict. As the bulldozer went about its demolition work ('We're gonna roll the motorway on'), the tumbling walls exposed characters from the past who led the audience into situations from the city's history which bore helpful similarities to the struggle of the contemporary community. One of these was 'Half-Hangit Maggie Dickson' who, having been 'hanged' in 1724 in Edinburgh's Grassmarket for the alleged murder of her child, was found by her pall-bearers, having taken their refreshment at a Craigmillar hostelry on the way to her burial place, to be still alive. Her song, 'I'm alive!' reflected the local community's own hopes.

Another historical echo, illustrating how human beings could become 'expendable', was the folk memory still alive in Newcraighall, a former mining village now part of the community, of how at a christening a child used to be 'arled', or bound for life, to the owner of the coal mine in which the local people laboured ('The arled bairn'). A lifetime of oppression followed. Women and children were disfigured by the long stooping hours of labour – the 'Niddrie lip', a facial disfiguration caused by years of hauling heavy carts, was said to be characteristic of local women. Men who broke away would find it almost impossible to find livelihood, such was the hold and influence of the owners and employers. These and other pictures from the past gave support and hope for the present.

This 'rocking torrent of a show' (Scotsman) was the first of the annual productions to use Richmond Craigmillar Church as a community theatre. The ring road was built – but took a different route.

This is the archetypal success show for a neighbourhood event … an undeniable hit. – Scotsman

We're gonna roll!

Chorus

We're gonna roll (we're gonna roll),
We're gonna roll (we're gonna roll),
We're gonna roll the motorway on.
(Repeat)

1. One fine day
they're gonna pull your house down.
One fine day
you'll find you're
out on the
street with your
dog and your cat and your old armchair.
Chorus

2. Now's the time
to build for the future.
Never mind
friendships you
say that you
knew in the
streets and the shops and the common stair!
Chorus

3. Motor car -
everybody wants one.
Don't you let
days gone by
stand in the
way of the
'right' of everyone to drive from door to door.
Chorus

I'm alive!

ad lib.
I'm a - live! Can it be no more dark-ness there for me?
1. You can't keep a good wo-man down.
The news is all ov-er the town.
They tried but they failed to have Mag-gie jailed un-der-ground, un-der-ground.
Sha-la, sha-la-la-la. Sha-la, sha-la - la-la.
v. 3 repeat ad lib.
Last time
Sha-la - la-la. Sha-la-la.

I'm alive!
Can it be
no more darkness
there for me?

1. You can't keep a good woman down,
the news is all over the town.
They tried but they failed
to have Maggie jailed
underground.
Shala, shalala …

2. You officials and lawyer men who
hold us down with your tired ballyhoo:
it takes ordinary folk
to show that the joke
is on you! …

3. You can't keep old Craigmillar down.
The news is all over the town.
We're over the top
and we're not going to stop
till we're there! …

The arled bairn

Daughter

1 Oh, Faither dear, it grieves me sair,
the tears fa' frae ma e'e,
that Ah should slave and be sae puir;
Ah feel like for tae dee.

2 Ah'm arled tae ma Maister's pit:
why did ye this tae me?
Fifteen lang 'oors' each day at it,
deep down below the sea.

3 Cauld, rak and dank the wark Ah dae,
wi' little pey tae show.
Ah nivver see the sun's bright ray -
why did Ah have tae go?

Father

4 My lass, Ah've lo'ed ye a' ma heart
frae yer baptismal day,
when first Ah signed the waefu' chart
tae arle ye for aye.

5 A collier's lot has little tae't
but poverty and death.
Masel' Ah'm chockit wi' the spit
and struggle hard for breath.

6 God kens, my lass, wi' ither five
sic bairns as you tae feed,
yet pay tae keep us a' alive
is aye in dreadfu' need.

7 Don't fau't yer Faither for the crime
that slaves ye tae the pit.
It's jist the system o' oor time
and we've tae struggle wi' it.

Daughter

8 But Faither, ither bairns are free
and dae nae work ava.
Why should this be the fate for me
and no' the fate for a'?

9 Ma face is white, me e'en are gray,
ma body's hackit sair;
Ah'm auld afore ma weddin' day
and scant o' claes tae wear.

10 There's lots o' lassies such as me
what struggle at the coals
and haul them tae the surface scree
thro' laigh and watery holes.

11 When crawling in the darkened mine
Ah pray tae God above
tae tak' me frae this cruel grind
tae his domain o' love.

Father

12 Such is the lot for us, my lass,
in bondage till we dee;
but shairly it will come tae pass
when colliers shall be free!

Castle, Cooncil and Curse 1974

This year's musical took housing as its theme. The plot arose from the frustration of local people at the long waiting list for houses, and a conviction that lack of will on the part of the authorities had prevented a large number of local flats from being repaired and made ready for occupancy (600 was the estimate), forcing young couples to live with parents and in-laws as well as 'stranding' old people in blocks of flats where most units lay unoccupied.

600 happened also to be the age, that year, of the local Craigmillar Castle, now a well-preserved ruin. The story begins with two officials (one from the Council, one from the castle) sharing complaints over a pint – one that he couldn't find a use for the castle, the other about the families badgering him for a house. They decided to help each other out by letting the castle out to the first family on the list. The typical extended family (plenty of chances for intergenerational tensions and humour) moved in reluctantly to this national monument ("kin we no git anything better!")

However, Mary the castle ghost was very unhappy about the new tenants and she decided to get rid of them. So the scary past of the castle starts to unfold before their eyes – Sir Simon Preston in the time of Edward 'the hammer of the Scots' forced to walk barefoot to London when the castle was taken in an English raid; Mary Queen of Scots signing Darnley's death warrant; Red Jess the witch – a woman of vision misunderstood; the earl murdered in his bath, and a host of others, their various trials and triumphs in counterpoint to the struggle of the present-day community to transform the neighbourhood.

The musical contains the song 'Craigmillar Now', written during a landmark meeting some months before between the Craigmillar Festival Society and representatives from the local City Council and the University of Edinburgh's Department of Urban Planning, an early example of consultation between local government and a local community. 'When the people play their part', written for this show, also made an appearance in 'Culture Vulture' in 1977.

... this roystering dynamic comedy ... wittily written,
well produced entertainment with a message
– Times Educational Supplement for Scotland, 28.6.74

Build me a castle

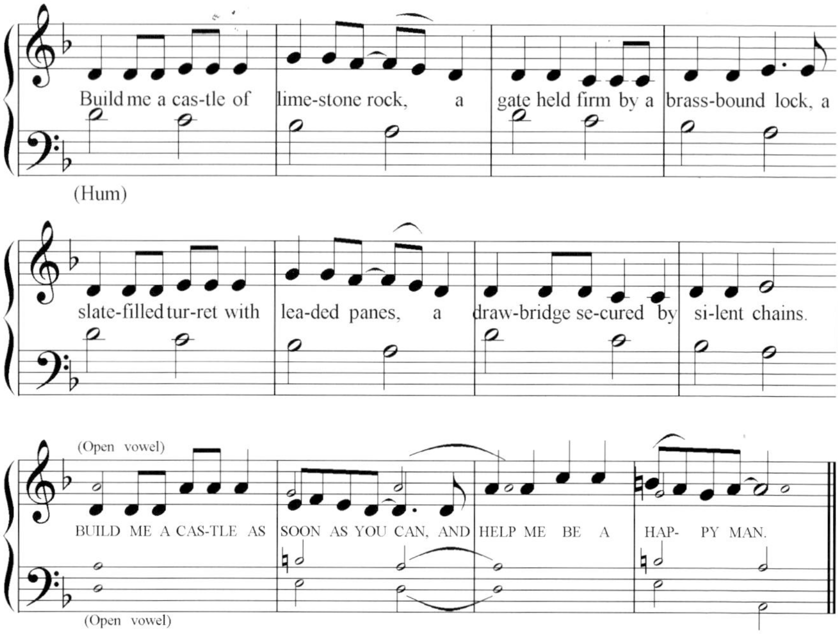

Build me a castle of limestone rock,
a gate held firm by a brass-bound lock,
a slate-tiled turret with leaded panes,
a drawbridge secured by silent chains.
BUILD ME CASTLE AS SOON AS YOU CAN
AND HELP ME TO BE A HAPPY MAN.

Fill my cellars with casks of wine;
hang my walls with tapestry fine;
a choice of mistress to grace my bed;
a costume embroidered with golden thread …

Fifty servants to meet my wishes
cuisine prepared on platinum dishes
and in my hall a throne of gold
inlaid with precious stones …

Three score old Masters in gilded frames
(none but the most impressive names)
even the chimneypiece must be
of silver hammered filigree.

Behind, a garden of richest green
where all the most cultured blooms may be seen
and round about, a twenty foot wall
built to the edge of a twenty foot fall …

Don't let's hang around

Chorus

Don't let's hang around, move it along!
Man the battlements, take it by storm.
You can make it
just the kind of
place where every-
one will want to belong.

1. Preston and his men of steel,
Mary and her lover,
jilted on midsummer's day
she never recovered …

2. A curse upon these dismal towers,
both you and all who follow.
May all who dwell within these walls
know nothing but sorrow …

3. An earl murdered as he bathes,
his blood pours in a torrent;
Mary Queen of Scots you'll see
sign a death warrant …

4. Red Jess the witch is next on trial
before a crowd unruly;
at the stake in anguished screams
she suffers most cruelly …

5. Then there is the family,
no roof to call their own;
a castle for a council house
is their new home …

He promised me

Words and music: Douglas Galbraith

mar-ry me,
that I would be your bride,
al-ways by your side,
be your joy and pride
ev-ery day, ev-ery way come what
may.
You
gradually fading
pro-mised me,
oh yes, you
pro - mised me.
repeat at lib.
Last time
You
pro - mised me.

He promised me,
oh yes, he promised me
that he would marry me,
that I would be his bride,
always by his side, be his joy and pride
every day, every way, come what may.

He promised me,
oh yes, he promised me
we'd never disagree;
and when our children came
we would still remain lovers just the same,
every day, every way, come what may.

Now he's gone and left me and I'm all alone;
there's no use in living when your loving man has gone.

> Why have you done this to me?
> Why treat me so cruelly?
> How could you do this to me?

You promised me,
oh yes, you promised me
that you would marry me,
that I would be your bride,
always by your side, be your joy and pride
every day, every way, come what may.

You promised me, oh yes, you promised me.
You promised me, oh yes, you promised me.

Rock and roll star

Little darlin' can't you see me goin' down London way.
(Shoobedoowa, shoobedoowah)
I tried to contact you before I went away.
(Shoobedoowa, shoobedoowah)
I can go by bus, by air, or even by car.
(Shoobedoowa, shoobedoowah)
It really doesn't matter 'cos I'm gonna be a rock 'n' roll star.
(Shoobedoowa, shoobedoowah)

Chorus

> Bless my soul, when I rock and roll
> I never know which way to run.
> I wanna see you when I rock and roll,
> I wanna see you when it's your turn.
> It's true I got the makin' just to be a rock 'n' roll star.
> (Shoobedoowa, shoobedoowah)

People will flock around just to see me go …
They come from miles around just to see a rock 'n' roll show …
I play my guitar and they sit and cuddle around …
Listenin' to the music, as they all enjoy the sound …

Chorus

And when the show is over I can stand back and hear them cheer …
They all shout for more and say won't you come back here …
A man said to me, Son, don't you know that you can go far …
And I say, Mister, all I want's to be's a Rock 'n' Roll star …

Chorus

Rock and roll (ad lib to fade)

When the people play their part

We thought the day had come
when we'd win through at last,
when all would walk with dignity
in their own cities, proud and free –
but now the moment's passed.

Chorus

The powerful in the land
can't bring a change of heart,
but history will be made
when the people play their part.

You ask me why I'm sad;
have you been on a trip!
The headlines stare you in the face,
and kidnap, killings, riot, race
hold us in their grip.

Chorus

But some say that they've heard
a whisper in the wind;
communities are on the move
their way of living to improve –
and festivals you'll find!

Chorus

Craigmillar now

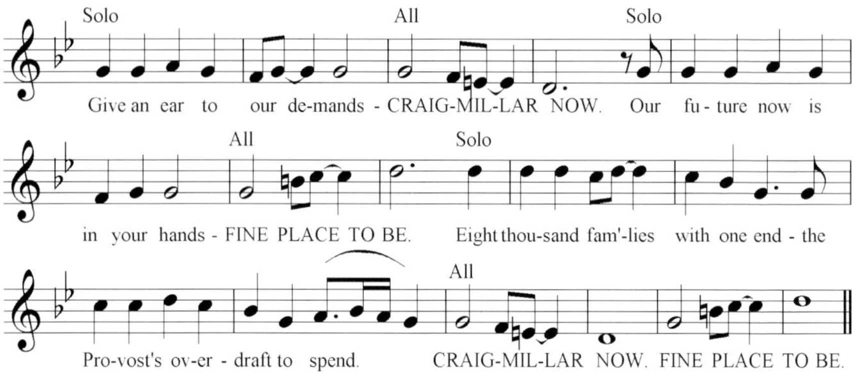

Give an ear to our demands – **Craigmillar now**
Our future now is in your hands – **fine place to be!**
Eight thousand families with one end
the Provost's overdraft to spend.
Craigmillar now, fine place to be!

An equal chance for each child born … **Craigmillar now**
For parents too a chance to learn … **fine place to be!**
Adventure playgrounds on the way
to practise living as we play …
Craigmillar now, fine place to be!

Old and young to live together … **Craigmillar now**
Neighbours not strangers to each other … **fine place to be!**
A house for every family
surroundings fine for all to see …
Craigmillar now, fine place to be!

Give us centres, home from home … **Craigmillar now**.
that we won't need the streets to roam … **fine place to be!**
Help us find some work to do,
have festival the whole year through …
Craigmillar now, fine place to be!

TIME & MOTION

Time and Motion Man 1975

This musical was inspired by a true incident in the 1950s when some local tattie howkers (potato pickers) saw and reported an unidentified flying object in the early morning sky. Another starting point was the impending visit from officials from the European Economic Community who were considering Craigmillar as a pilot community for a grant-aided research and action programme where the initiative would remain in local hands rather than with government.

In the musical, the *Time and Motion Man*, the 'super researcher' arrives by space ship to monitor the district from the perspective of the future, especially observing a typical family, that of Wattie Deans, a redundant miner who while tattie picking had spotted his craft. He follows the Deans family back to their origin in the caves, where his ancestors practised their art on the walls, played their music on bones and hunted wild animals. On through to the Roman times, when the first recognisable Wattie was sired by a Roman soldier building Brunstane Bridge and whose mother was a maiden from the local Votadina tribe (note the pun). In the Industrial Revolution, father, mother and bairns all worked in the pits, while the Wattie of 1926 suffered hardship during the General Strike.

The researcher is able to show the family their past, but also what the future could hold. For audience, cast and community, the musical offers two options, remaining trapped in the ways of the past or choosing a new future.

The show was vigorous and vital, full of humour and pathos.
– Times Educational Supplement for Scotland, 04.07.75

Alas, my true love

Words and music: Douglas Galbraith

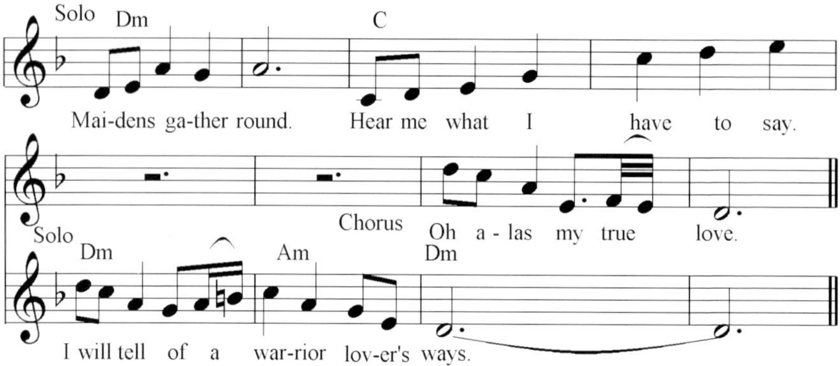

(Solo, all sing last line)

Maidens gather round,
hear me what I have to say.
I will tell of a warrior lover's ways.
Oh, alas, my true love.

Whispering your name,
he will promise ne'er to part,
but to prove his love he'll break your heart.
Oh, alas, my true love.

Thrill of steel on steel
will be meat and drink to him.
Food will turn to ashes in your mouth.
Oh, alas, my true love.

'I give you my word,
I will never make you weep',
they will swear but their promise cannot keep.
Oh, alas, my true love.

Wattie Deans

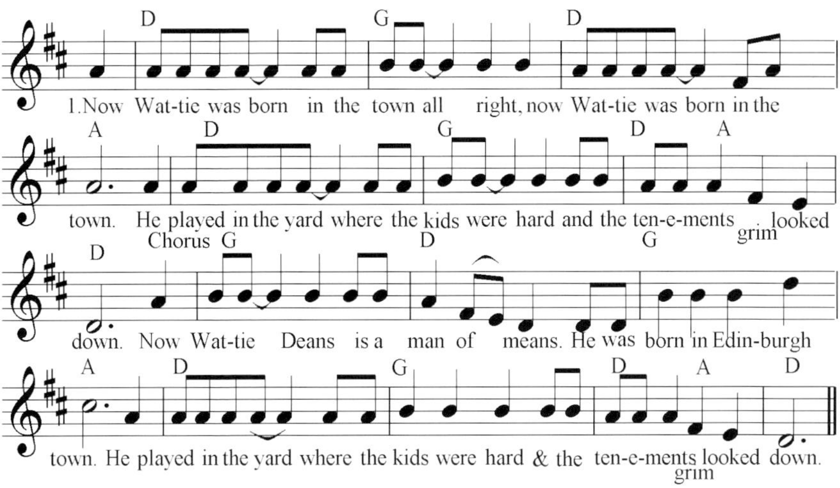

Now Wattie was born in the town all right,
now Wattie was born in the town.
He played in the yard where the kids were hard
and the tenements grim looked down.

Chorus

> Now Wattie Deans is a man of means.
> He was born in Edinburgh town.
> He played in the yard where the kids were hard
> and the tenements grim looked down.

Now Wattie thought that he should be taught
the cup of wisdom how to drink.
So he went to school to learn the rule;
repeat after me, Don't think …

So Wattie went down the mine all right,
so Wattie went down the mine.
But he wanted to live in the country bright
and breathe the air so fine …

The wages to lift are six bob a shift,
with not a place to wash.
So Wattie was glad when the world went mad
and he went to fight the Boche …

When he returned the wealth had gone
and the heroes they were dead.
Cold depression froze, the mine had to close;
the country was in the red …

So Wattie went out to look for work
for his family needed to be fed.
But a job is gold and at last he was told
to join the queue for bread.

We're in orbit

Chorus

We're in orbit, we are climbing through space,
seeking a new kind of place.
We're in motion, – who can stand in our way? –
nearer the target each day.

Wattie Deans, where have you been,
to and fro in the time machine?
Sharing a pad with a pterodactyl
doesn't seem the way to get away from it all …

Down below digging the coal,
caked in dust from head to toe.
Up above the sun shines bright,
but Wattie and his children never see the light …

Wattie Deans now trying on
the uniform of centurion.
Meets a maid on the side of a hill;
although she's a Briton he's not prejudiced at all! …

Present day, Deans on the dole,
feels the government owns his soul.
'What's the use! Things won't improve.
What do you mean it's me to make the next move?' …

[and at end of show]

Wattie Deans, where have you been
to and fro in the time machine?
What have you found in your travels through time?
You can play the system if you make up your mind? …

Wattie Deans, over to you,
you've got the power if you take your cue.
Don't leave it to the folk at the top;
it is your own future that we're talking about …

Time and motion man

Watching over the universe, coming down from the stars,
making rings round Saturn, Jupiter and Mars.
I've come down to show you what needs to be done;
feel the heat of the sun, feel the heat of the sun.

I'm the time and motion man,
gonna help you if I can.
I'm the time and motion man,
gonna help you if I can.

Like a glowing comet flashing through the sky,
sliding through the stratosphere faster than the eye.
I've come down to show you what needs to be done;
feel the heat of the sun, feel the heat of the sun.

I'm a super researcher.
I'm not going to letcha
do what you wanna do.
I've got the answer,
and there's no chance ya'll
find your own way through.

this verse spoken over the music
I've come down to help you, you're weak and I'm strong.
I know you think you're right, but I know you're wrong.
I'm the king, I know everything, I'll tell you what to be.
So don't say you'll do it your way; just sit there and listen to me.

I'm the time and motion man

Say but the future

Words and music: Bell/Dick

Say, but the future looks bright
now that we all see the light.
The time and motion man he will be there,
giving us all the answers.
Tomorrow will work out just fine.
We will say ‘ours’ not ‘mine’.
Now every new day will be a happy one –
say, but the future looks bright.

Say, but the future looks clear,
because of what we see and hear.
The time and motion man he will be there,
giving us all the answers.
Saying goodbye to the past,
live for a new day at last.
Now every new day will be a happy one –
say, but the future looks bright.

When your fathers tasted bitterness

Words: Andrew Crummy
Music: Douglas Galbraith

When your fathers tasted bitterness
the children felt their teeth were set on edge;
when nobody loved your mother
it was you who knew the thin end of the wedge.
How to stop the world turning
and watch the shadow fall
on the same place upon the prison wall?

When you're tired of living underground
and all the folk you speak to feel the same;
when the men who know the answers
know just everything about you but your name.
How to stop the world turning
and watch the shadow fall
on the same place upon the prison wall?

Step outside your narrow orbit,
making partners of the people with the power;
with your artist's hand put things together
in a way that didn't fit before.
Turn statistics to compassion and graphs to human face,
and teach everybody longer memories.

What kind of love?

can
I
not
1 get you out of my mind?
2 stop
think - ing a - bout you?
D.C.
Coda
gradually fading

How can you come
talking of love
when your eyes flash
fire and murder,
pillage and destruction?

What kind of love
burns down my home,
takes my brothers,
uncles, lovers,
before my very eyes?

Why can I not get you out of my mind?
Why can I not stop thinking about you?

How can you come
talking of love
when your eyes flash
fire and murder,
pillage and destruction?

Why do I still
come back to you?
Is there no-one
of my own kind
can satisfy my longings?

Rehabilitation

Solo Along came a man with a long degree.
All *Rehabilitation!*
Solo He said, I bet you're glad to see me!
All *Rehabilitation!*
Solo I've come to put your house to rights,
All *Rehabilitation!*
Solo rip out the bath and put out the lights.
All *Rehabilitation!*

Rehabilitation, rehabilitation,
rehabilitation, that's the name of the game!

On Monday they took my old front door …
On Tuesday they made a hole in the floor …
Wednesday they bored right through the wall …
On Thursday they did sweet damn all …

Put your house in order, put your house in order,
put your house in order, that's the name of the game!

Oh the cold runs hot and the hot runs cold …
and the cooker's down in the garden below …
They've changed all the sockets before I could wink …
and they've joined all the wires to the kitchen sink …

This is really living, this is really living,
this is really living, that's the name of the game!

New wallpaper and a roof repair …
Who cares if you don't like it here …
Remove the midden, sow a few seeds …
Who cares about your leisure needs! …

Bring a new tomorrow, bring a new tomorrow,
bring a new tomorrow, that's the name of the game!

Put some paint on the ceiling, clean the slogans off the stair …
A touch of paint put here and there …
How could a person ever want for more? …
but when I look outside it's still 1934 …

Rehabilitation, rehabilitation,
rehabilitation, that's the name of the game!

That year, a National Children's Bureau report published disturbing statistics to show that in Scotland one in every ten children was disadvantaged. For Craigmillar, this was more than just a statistic.

In the musical, one of those is Willie Wynn, now six years further on aged 17 and facing adulthood – but with what? He has no job, no prospects, and no expectations of himself either, one of the lost generation, a no-hoper, 'born to fail' – well, not quite. For Willie copes with life by means of colourful fantasies.

The story tells how gang member Willie deals with his problems. Father in jail, mounting family debts, electricity cut off, facing eviction, rejected by school, by neighbours and by society at large, he calls on his vivid imagination, his quick wit and sense of fun. He is able to conjure up a different world, involving his family and friends. At the end of a year on the Youth Opportunity Programme, Willie Wynn (again, note the pun) stands for the possibility that the cycle of deprivation can be broken, carried through by people's belief in themselves and their visions for the future.

The message to the community was that its most precious asset was its high proportion of children and young people, and that to realise this asset there was a need for bolder educational provision with the important addition of local community encouragement and nurture. They sang, 'Imagination more and to spare; hang on to us and we'll take you there'.

The community musical is always a centrepiece of Craigmillar's annual festival in Edinburgh, operating on a simple formula which requires the participation of approximately half of Craigmillar's population …

(The) fantasy sequences were written, directed and performed by the staff and pupils of separate schools. The most effective were a 'Pop Star' fantasy by Castlebrae Secondary, which turned out to be almost satirical, and 'Fairyland' by St. Francis Primary …

Lusty and spirited songs were performed in a lusty and spirited fashion, and from time to time there was good backing by a rock group called Denim, who were, at their best, sensitive and thoughtful. – Scotsman

Yesterday

1. Yes - ter - day I dreamed a dream or so
of a boy who used to pass my door,
used to watch un - til he reached the street -
saw him no

Words: Douglas Galbraith, music: Andrew Crummy

Yesterday I dreamed a dream or so
of a boy who used to pass my door.
Used to watch until he reached the street –
saw him no more.

Waited for him walking back again,
different in a way I can't explain,
till one day he looked across at me;
I knew it then.

They will try to tell us we are wrong,
try to say to us we don't belong,
but I've never felt so sure before
of anyone.

There was a time

Words and music: Douglas Galbraith

There was a time
when I lived each day and thought of nothing.
There was a time
when I wove and spun and reaped and sowed
and cleaned and turned the soil
and thought of nothing.
The ground in which I grew was hard and bare and cold;
I didn't know that anything could become of me.

He came to me,
and I felt his gaze reach deep inside me.
He sang to me
and my heart began to open like the lily flower
that blooms in highest summer.
He showed to me a self I didn't know was there;
I went about, glad in his love, bathed in his sun.

There came a time
when he turned from me to be a soldier.
There came a time
when I watched him go and talked of all the things
we'd do when all the fighting's over.
And when the cursing, crying, gasping air was still
they found him there, mid the lilies fair, as they touched his hair.

Favourite band

I'm thinking about my favourite band.
It ain't Suzy Quatro carrying the can.
It ain't the Rollers shanging a lang.
It's a band that I'm in,
a little band that's called Denim.
They're the greatest thing on earth:
play from here to Perth.

And every time I think of us,
imagine our name scrawled on a bus
– much bigger than the Beatles or the Who's Magic Bus.
It's a band, my favourite band,
even bigger than Jimmy Shand.
And even Slade ain't got a thing on them;
the band's name is Denim.

I know, I can feel it in my heart
that I'm a star,
a superstar, superstar, superstar.

I can't take my mind off my favourite band.
Do gigs all over, just one night stands.
It isn't Slick or even Tom Jones' brand.
It's a band that I'm in,
a little band that's called Denim.
They're the greatest thing on earth:
play from here to Perth.

I know, I can feel it in my heart
that I'm a star,
a superstar, superstar, superstar.

More of us than you!

Chorus

Look at your children, we'll tell you true;
you'd better listen, for there's
very many
more of us than
you!

Concrete straitjacket, for a necklace a Yale;
no-one to listen, born to fail …

You put the question, we'll tell you no lie;
the answer's around you before your very eye …

Know where we come from, know who we are;
the secret is buried in your own back yard …

Imagination more and to spare;
hang on to us and we will take you there …

Bury our talents and you'll rue the day;
try to ignore us – we just won't go away …

Fresh as the morning, fresh is our view;
please do not bore us till we talk like you …

Think of this, please, when you leave us today;
we are the ones who can show you the way …

Circle of life

Mr. Smith –
why do you stay in the town you were born in,
with the walls closing in and the factory dying?
Cooking pan, tally man,
sick dad, growing lad.
Can't break the chains, and it's no use trying.

What's gonna happen when your kids get older?
Will their magazine dreams gather dust like yours?
Shining home, coloured phone,
social whirl, glamour girl
drowned in the sink with the household chores.

Mr. Jones –
why do you travel on the packed 8.40,
frowning at the pages in the business news?
Falling pound, shares down,
school fees, mortgages;
fifty other people trying to fill your shoes.

What's gonna happen when your kids get older?
Will they fall into a life like yours?
Pin-stripe, back-snipe,
daren't stop, near top.
Will they have a choice, will they open the doors?

spoken or improvised over instrumental backing
Will they ever get to choose their own life,
are they free to go their own way?
Will they ever break the circle?
Will they stray?

Mr. Smith –
the future's looking good, it ain't so bad.
Come along now, and don't be sad.
Family life, no more strife,
helping hand, understand;
people join together and all hold hands.

Your magazine dreams, they are all lies;
life is what you make it, if you'd only realise.
Happy days, friendly ways,
sunshine, all mine.
They can have a choice, they can open doors,
they can stray.

The terror men

Words: Johnni Stanton, music: Douglas Galbraith

O we lead the field, there is nobody like us;
for we are out in front, there is no-one to touch us
'cos we've got what it takes, we jan the style:
the gear that we wear, by our denims we swear.
We'll say it again and again and again:
we're the Terror Men.

O we're unemployed and we cannae get jobs
so we all sit back and watch 'Top of the Pops'.
We might hang around with a pint in the pub,
and after a while go to the Hut Club.
We'll say it again and again and again:
we're the Terror Men.

O we've had trouble with cops and wee greasy chip shops;
We smash a' the windaes where the 21 stops.
We've been at the Court, we laugh at the Law;
if you get in our way, we'll spray paint on your wa'.
We'll say it again and again and again:
we're the Terror Men.

This musical was about two festivals, the international Edinburgh Festival where it was possible to 'enjoy art' as a consumer and the Craigmillar Festival where the arts were bedded in the issues which faced people living in a community which still had to cope with disadvantages. Did the Edinburgh festivalgoer, coming from outside, see the whole picture? 'What have you come to see? – you look right through me ...' How to achieve the balance in economic priorities between supporting the arts and tackling deprivation? The musical had its own point of view, that the balance was not yet right.

Nevertheless, the two festivals had important things in common. Both set high store by the arts, on the creativity of people, on embracing new possibilities through the media of music, drama, painting, sculpture and the rest. The local festival even had its advantages in that people could enjoy a cultural life all the year round in the provisions that were made through the Festival Society and others. The message of the musical was, 'Don't waste these opportunities. Nourished and tended with care, the roots of the plant and the rare blossoms that stem from it already will grow even more beautiful and multiply, so that there will be enough for all to enjoy – not just the élitist few.'

For 30p there are not many places left where one can witness a festival of art, opera, history, rock, and a miniature version of the military tattoo in one evening – and find oneself in the middle of the terracings of Edinburgh's Easter Road into the bargain ...

About 80 children from schools in the area are used to great effect – probably because nobody asked them to wear awkward stage costumes or adopt particular accents. Their singing is powerful, tuneful and clear ...

The professional actors add polish to the show, but do not mask the natural talent of the 'rough diamonds' ... Another performance which does not quickly fade from the memory is a beautiful rendering of ... 'When the people play their part' by Janet Howie, who is blind ...

The production has its imperfections and sharp edges – but they are those of handcrafted pottery which loses none of its charm because of them.
– Scotsman

Time for change

Words: Johnni Stanton, music: Joe Brown

I doubt that you could show me
just how my life should be.
I doubt that you could help me
to be free, to be free.

Throw away all you gave to me,
your values mean nothing at all.
Don't want no part in your society,
'cause one day it's gonna fall.

I doubt that you could show me
just how my life should be.
I doubt that you could help me
to be free, to be free.

Let us all be free to be
what we want our lives to be.

Culture vulture

Culture vulture, what have you come to see?
Culture vulture, you look right through me,
turn my city topsy turvy.
Why come and bother me?
Why can't you leave me be?

Culture vulture, what have you come to see?
Culture vulture, my rent and rates they
confiscate, so jam you'll eat.
You will go on the binge,
leaving me on the Fringe!

Trio Performance we seek
seven days in the week
with a Diamand-studded cast.
With our seats booked last March,
we have come here to gorge –
put some life in your city at last!

Verses 1 and 2 are repeated

Trio We will miss not a show
(though at home we don't go),
symphony, morning concert, late revue.
Ballet is my delight, (*Voice 1*)
mine is opera each night – (*Voice 2*)
the discriminating few!

Chorus
Won't you look in our direction;
is there no connection
with what you're seeking?
Each and everyone an artist,
working with whatever's at hand.

Chorus is repeated

Culture vulture, what have you come to see?
Culture vulture, I might have guessed –
only the best, ignore the rest. But
how can you pluck a bloom
save from a plant that's strong?

Chorus is sung twice

Can it be?

Solo
I go to a place.
Search e - very face.
Could it be him?
I walk in the street.
Scan-ning the fa-ces of

Words and music: Douglas Galbraith

kind.
I walk in the
street,
scan-ning fa-ces of those
the
that I meet.
Could it be him?
I won-der if
3

ad lib.
that man is like him at all?
Reading the news, giving his views, filling the pews,
or de - cor -a-ting a wall.
I go to a place.
Search ev-ery face.

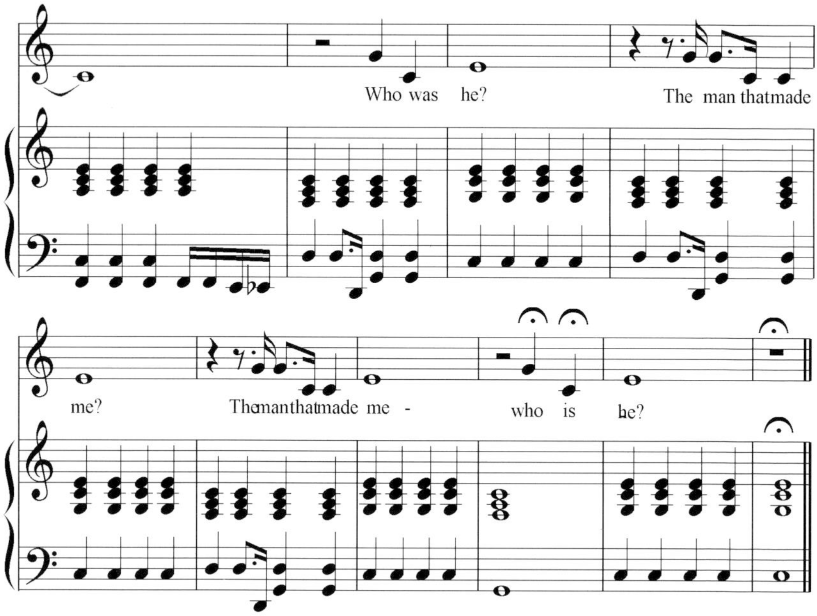
Who was he?
The man that made me?
The man that made me - who is he?

I go to a place,
search every face;
could it be him?

I walk in the street
scanning the faces of those that I meet;
could it be him?

> You and me
> don't add up to three.
> Something inside
> reaches for its own kind.

I walk in the street
scanning the faces of those that I meet;
could it be him?

> I wonder if
> that man was like him at all –
> reading the news, giving his views, filling the pews
> or decorating a wall.

I go to a place,
search every face;
who was he –
the man that made me?
The man that made me – who was he?

Alice Henderson and Johnni Stanton

On the fringe of the Edinburgh Festival

Castle for a King (1976)

This was a pageant played out in the rooms, halls and courtyards of Craigmillar Castle, which told the story of the castle in words and music. The plot was based on the life and times of King James V, father of Mary Queen of Scots. The twelve year old James is taken to the castle to escape the Black Death, and the action ranges back to the marriage of his father James IV and Margaret Tudor, sister of Henry VIII. It recalled their journey through the district on the way to their wedding in Edinburgh and the king's visit to the castle before his death at Flodden in 1513.

The play took the form of a conducted tour, with the guide's lists of dates and royal occasions soon broken into by the charlady who offers an alternative take on the same events, from the point of view of the ordinary people involved. Chrissie the cleaner then becomes the equally lively Kirsty, a serving woman during the residence of James IV. To help her recreate the worries, hopes and loves of the ordinary people of the time, she raises the somewhat unwilling ghosts of her erstwhile contemporaries – tumblers, minstrels, fire-eaters, nobles and the occasional monarch.

'Castle for a King' was first performed in Lothian Heritage Week (May 1976) with the participation in the cast of three local councillors, but it was also written against the backdrop of grant negotiations with the EEC. The relevance of the play was described by Helen Crummy: 'King James IV showed concern for his people and did two very important things. He introduced culture from outside Scotland, particularly from France, and this can be compared with what we are trying to do for Craigmillar and Edinburgh by means of our European Economic Community grant. He also introduced fishing and farming projects, similar to EEC attempts to attract new industries by the placing of their grants'.

The material was incorporated in the community musical of that year and the play was again performed as part of the Edinburgh Festival Fringe.

The basic narrative is frequently interrupted by some very good songs and music ... overall a very refreshing show – Festival Times 25.08.76

Unpretentious and entertaining and a thoroughly worth-while venture. – Scotsman 27.08.76

Why rade ye forth?

Words: Ian Cowie, music: 'Whigs awa", Scottish trad.

Oh black's the day, foul black's the day
when ye rade forth, O Jamie.
For noo oor land is sad and wae;
why rade ye forth, O Jamie?

Tae Flodden's field ye rade and died,
when ye rade forth, O Jamie.
The floo'er o' men lie at your side;
why rade ye forth, O Jamie?

And aye we telt ye no' tae gang,
when ye rade forth, O Jamie.
Ower late ye fund that ye were wrang;
why rade ye forth, O Jamie?

Braw Huntly, Lennox, Crawford, Mar,
when ye rade forth, O Jamie.
But noo they're happit in the glaur;
why rade ye forth, O Jamie?

The fire and sword sweep through oor land,
when ye rade forth, O Jamie.
And Scotland's noo in England's hand;
why rade ye forth, O Jamie?

Sae sair we greet for glory died,
when ye rade forth, O Jamie.
The croon ill fits an orphan's heid;
why rade ye forth, O Jamie?

Herald's song

Words: Douglas Galbraith and Johnni Stanton, music 'Balulalow', Scottish trad.

Oh come with me and let me show
to you what happened long ago.
For you today I'll bring to life
a tale of love, intrigue and strife,
of a good king, Jamie by name,
fourth of that line of lasting fame.
He gave this land a greater pride, a greater pride;
all Scotland prospered till he died.

But you must hear me first of all
tell of the Stewart in this hall,
and by his side a princess fair,
of feature pale and red of hair,
the daughter of the Tudor court,
to share a Scottish bed and board.
Now will two nations find repose, will find repose,
that joinèd be the Thistle and Rose.

Now must I take you ten year's hence,
when England's king sailed ower tae France,
against oor nation's ancient friend;
a turquoise ring their Queen did send,
pleading that James would be her Knight,
take up his banners for the right.
The gallant Stewart kept his pledge, he kept his pledge;
two armies met at Flodden edge.

O mother speak

Words: Douglas Galbraith, music 'Balulalow', Scottish trad.

Child:

O mother speak and tell me true
why I should aye live far from you.
Why is't that those who power have won
should part a mother from her son?
One stranger bids me to rise,
another stranger soothes my cries
as when my stumbling limb is torn, my limb is torn
upon the thistle or the thorn.

Yet mother dear, why should I crave
for more than many children have,
with those around me who can give
the things to help me fully live?
Singing of days now past and gone,
telling of marvels still to come –
I would all bairns surrounded be, surrounded be,
with such as greatly care for me.

Mother:

Sweet prince, I bid you take your rest.
May gentlest sleep be now your guest;
no fitful fancy plague your head,
but pleasing dreams attend your bed.
Dream of the day you will hunt the roe,
following the chase where none would go.
When comes the day your throne ascend
to you all men the knee will bend

30
YEARS OF
CRAIGMILLAR COMMUNITY
MUSICALS

On the fringe of the Edinburgh Festival

The Craigmillar Recipe (1977)

Under threat, not for the first time in its life, from financial cutbacks, the Craigmillar Festival Society published in dramatic form its recipe for survival in a show written by John Milligan. Just as a haggis needs a variety of ingredients, a community needs the richness and diversity of talent found in the people of the district – 'a touch of this, a shake of that, then throw in everything you've got'. To take any part of this away threatens the whole and destroys the taste. The show made its point; the CFS survived.

An impressive piece of political theatre at its most immediate.
– Scotsman

Haggis roundel

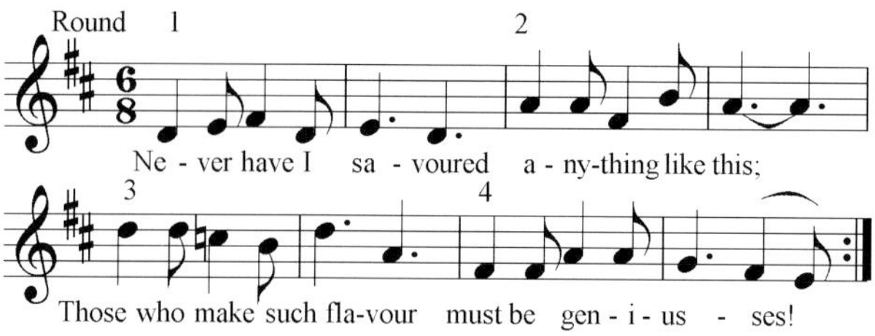

Haggis song

Take the paunch of a sheep,
take its heart, lungs and liver;
all these things you must keep, not waste.
Take some meal from your store,
onions, suet and spices to give taste.

Pepper palate to unsettle, onion appetite to whet'll
tempt you to a dish most rare.
Gravy mixing all together helps each part flavour the other,
share its riches everywhere.

Won't find a dish LIKE THIS!
What is its name? – HAGGIS!

Take the paunch of a sheep,
take its heart, lungs and liver;
all these things you must keep, not waste.
Take some meal from your store,
onions, suet and spices to give taste.

Here some oats from Niddrie Mains,
a pinch of salt from Prestonpans,
suet from the Magdalene.
Here we bring a piece of liver,
used to graze by Bingham's river,
heart from every but and ben.

Your gift of meat, EACH PIECE,
We'll change into A FEAST!

Take a handful of folk,
take some determination,
add a shake of some native wit.
If you give us the 'bread'
we will make it go further, each bit.

We have found a recipe, discovered in necessity,
but better than a prepacked meal:
a touch of this, a shake of that,
then throw in everything you've got
　　and double nourishment as well.

How can they kill HAGGIS!
How can they kill HAGGIS!

Fresh in the morning

Fresh the morning when I saw this place.
Fresh the grief I carried in my face.
Twelve-year memory saw my mother die and all my family,
hungrily.
Fresh the morning when they came for me.

Now I carry from the larder free
meat enough to fill my Lords and me;
in a special store food to give to those who live outside the door,
hunger o-er.
Thought I'd never fear for them any more.

Why should it be your way?
Why always your say?
Saving your meat
to squander the wisdom and wit
of the people who sit at your feet!

Fresh the morning …

Later community musicals

The tradition of annual community musicals continued after the years covered in this collection. A typical example was 'Shoo!', its starting point found in the reluctant realisation that for all the work of the Society and the skilful application of grant aid, not least a major EEC grant to try and nail the causes of poverty, the community seemed no nearer the solution. In her book about the Society, Helen Crummy quotes their annual report:

After five years of research into poverty, where is the evidence that those who hold the power, the purse, or dwell in ivory towers, are any nearer understanding what poverty really means in human terms? ... Nowhere in their formal reports is there room for humanising their facts and figures!

The musical was the story of a family of ten threatened with eviction from their council house who took up residence in a derelict toll house. Quickly they learned they had to keep out of sight. The farmer 'shooed' them off his land. The wider society had already successfully banished them from its sight. However, being near the airport, the children find that their road was being used to smuggle VIPs out of the airport by the back door. The plot thickened but the question remained at the end.

Excerpts from this musical appeared on the television film 'Open Door', attracting wide notice and causing considerable discussion. One of the songs, 'The Plenty', by the late Joe McGinley, then music director of the Festival, caught the theme, and is still sung in the community. It is included here as representative of the many other later songs, and perhaps as a trailer for a second volume of *Craigmillar Gold*!

The plenty

1. There was a time so long a- go when child-ren wan - dered
Cm7 F7 Cm7
emp- ty, but now the milk and hon - ey flow and
F7 Abmaj7 Dbmaj7
we share out the plen - ty. (Last time)
we share out the plen - ty.
GbGnat G7+C G7+C

Words and music: Joe McGinley

There was a time so long ago
when children wandered empty,
but now the milk and honey flow
and we share out the plenty.

Can we still taste those year-long nights
when people's hearts were tainted,
no need to kill, no need to fight,
for we share out the plenty.

It used to be that one had one,
the other he took twenty,
before we found ourselves a way
where we share out the plenty.

No air was breathed, no grass was seen,
no living things were planted,
but now our earth and sky are clean,
while we share out the plenty.

The people in this land were two,
the peasants and the gentry;
but mutual understandings grew
AS WE SHARE OUT THE PLENTY.

The Craigmillar Festival Society

WILL PRESENT AN

HISTORICAL PAGEANT AT CRAIGMILLAR CASTLE

ENTITLED

"CRAIGMILLAR: Castle for a King"

The Life and Times of King James V

FATHER OF

MARY, QUEEN OF SCOTS

Will Be Depicted In Words and Music

A TRUE TALE OF OLD SCOTLAND !!

ON MONDAY, 17 MAY AND WEDNESDAY, 19 MAY

Two Performances at 2.00 p.m. and 4.00 p.m.

First Coach Departs Waverley Bridge at 1.30 p.m.
(Returning to City at 4.00 p.m. approximately).

Second Coach Departs Waverley Bridge at 3.30 p.m.
(Returning to City at 6.00 p.m. approximately).

VISITORS WITH OWN TRANSPORTATION WELCOME

ENTRANCE FEE is only 15 pence, and includes admission to CASTLE. COACH is an additional 35 pence.